HOW TO LIVE WITH A NEUROTIC CAT OWNER

HOW TO LIVE WITH A NEUROTIC CAT OWNER

Everything you always wanted to know about your cat but were afraid to ask.
Everything your cat knows about you without even having to ask!

As told to Stephen Baker

Illustrated by Roger Roth

SOUVENIR PRESS

Ask not what your
cat can do for you . . .

CONTENTS

Does your cat own you?
Now you can understand the feline mind (very furry),
train your cat (ha!) and gain
the upper paw
(good luck!)

COMMAND → ← COMMAND

How to Live with

A

Neurotic

by Stephen Baker

INTRODUCTION

Why this book? It's high time, that's why. Most books on cats have been written by humans who may or may not know much about the subject at hand—the latter being a more likely possibility. Until now, no book on cats has been written by those who know best, the cats themselves.

I, the true author (never mind what it says on the cover) of this book, am eminently qualified to deliberate on the psyche of cat owners—a peculiar breed deserving as much attention as the animal they claim ownership of, if not more. My "owner"—note my quotation marks—happens to be the author of *How to Live with a Neurotic Cat*, a ridiculous piece of fluff of absolutely no literary merit, but which nevertheless captured the fancy of thousands of cat lovers the world over, if not one single cat (that should tell you something). I was given the unique opportunity to sit on his shoulder and watch the words flash on the word processor, an experience that caused me to walk away in dismay on numerous occasions and head straight for the kitchen, the best place yet to find solace.

Now it's my turn.

Part One

US, CATS

*Everything you ever wanted to know about
your cat
but thought you'd just as soon not ask.*

COMPATIBILITY TEST

Do you get along well with your cat? Or more importantly, how well does your cat get along with you? Take this test and find out.

	yes	no
1. Do you and your cat share the same taste in food?	☐	☐
2. Do you love your cat as much as your cat loves himself?	☐	☐
3. Do you give your cat a complete massage at least three times a day?	☐	☐
4. Do you have a special chair at the dining table set aside for your cat?	☐	☐
5. Do you help your cat fall asleep in the evening by singing his favourite lullabies?	☐	☐
6. Is your cat more important to you than your boss, wife, and children?	☐	☐
7. Do you leave enough room for your cat in bed at night—say, half the area or more?	☐	☐
8. Are you willing to go and sleep on the living room sofa if there is room for only one of you in your bed?	☐	☐
9. Do you and your cat enjoy the same television programmes?	☐	☐
10. Have you ever purposely kept your cat awake for more than ten minutes?	☐	☐

A "yes" answer to half or more of these questions shows there is hope. Less than half suggests you and your cat have yet to come to a firm understanding. You need help.

1

How Cats
Got That Way

Let's begin by setting the record straight. It is not us cats who are neurotic; our owners are.

And no wonder. Look at it this way: We joined the human race more than ten thousand years ago. We became part of the household, a member of the family, if you will. We would be there when needed, or even when not. Under the circumstances, our owners did the best they could. But the pressure must have got the better of them: They have become neurotic in the process.

One of the problems between us and our owners really goes back to a simple misunderstanding, and that is that cats can be tamed, even made to work for a living. A ridiculous concept? Of course it is. Yet, even today, there are those who believe the idea has merit.

The name *Felis domesticus* should tell you something. The scientists who came up with that name just didn't get it. They didn't have the foggiest idea what they were talking about. Many of them probably never even owned the cat. Or worse, they confused us with dogs. The words clearly suggest that we have been domesticated.

The most that could be said—a hundred-to-one shot, mind you—is that we are in the *process* of being domesticated. Note the difference. We're not there yet. But don't give up. Keep trying; give us a little more time. A few million more years just may do it.

To understand us cats, it is important to keep in mind our true origins, where we came from. We are creatures of the wild. For ever so long we tried to make it on our own. But it was a jungle out there. Giant creatures roamed the earth, chomping at the mouth looking for something to eat. They had insatiable appetites and were anything but choosy in their taste. Anything would do, even a cat. It came down to this: eat or be eaten. We preferred the former.

It was about this time that a new kind of species appeared on the landscape, the like of which we had never seen. It wasn't much to look at; he had a lot of hair around his chin and sometimes on top of his head, but not much elsewhere. He spoke in grunts, making no sense. But he walked on his hind legs unlike any other creature, which allowed him to carry sticks and stones with which to down animals several times his size, enough to serve a large family for days on end. Obviously, here was someone to be reckoned with. What the new arrival lacked in agility and intellect, not to mention common sense, he more than made up for in advanced weaponry and determination.

The creature caught our forefathers' attention at once. Their long-cherished dream had finally become a reality—the beginning of a New Age. At long last, here was someone offering room and board, free of charge.

First signs of civilisation:
the Blanket.

MAN'S MOST NOTEWORTHY CONTRIBUTIONS

Double Bed

Interior Spring Mattress

Rubbish Bin

Reclining Chair

Windowsills

Local Supermarket

Television

Not all owners are the same. Shown here are some we can do without.

Owners who eat everything on their plates

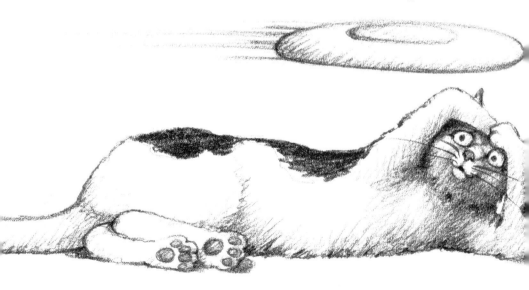

Owners who try teaching their cats to catch a Frisbee

Owners who want the bed all to themselves

Owners who write books on cats

Also: THOSE WHO USE THESE EXPRESSIONS:

"Not enough room to swing a cat."

"Cats always land on their feet."

"See which way the cat jumps."

"Curiosity killed the cat."

"Cats have nine lives."

AND *THE ONE TO AVOID AT ANY COST:*

"Cats are biodegradable."

2

How to Recognise a Cat

With so many new breeds being introduced year after year, it has become increasingly difficult to tell one kind of cat from another, or even recognise the species. Your state of confusion will come to an end when you've finished reading this chapter.

Forget what you've heard so far, books that insist on showing page after page of breeds—each with distinct markings, a unique personality, and a long line of ancestry all their own. This kind of information only complicates matters.

All you have to know is this: your cat's **size** and **shape.**

The distinctions between the five **Basic Breeds** shown on the following pages are founded on this simple premise. Commit the following to memory and you will soon be able to impress all your cat-loving friends with your profound knowledge of feline physiology.

Large Cat does not fit into the washbasin, perhaps not even the bathtub.

Small Cat is able to work his way into a biscuit barrel, if not out of it. Also fits inside slippers, handbag, or briefcase.

Round Cat resting on bed or living room sofa is often confused with a pillow to sit on.

Square Cat fits neatly into all corners: room, cupboard, drawers.

Tubular Cat has no problem reaching top of dining table, kitchen worktop, rubbish bin, or any other place you wish he would not be able to.

27

Length and type of **coat** offer additional clues to the breed you're dealing with.

Long Hair moults in spring, summer, autumn, winter and the rest of the year.

Short Hair shows more cat, less fur.

No Hair likes summer, hates winter.

Ignore all the anatomical drawings of cats you ever saw. The feline body is simplicity itself. This is all you have to remember:

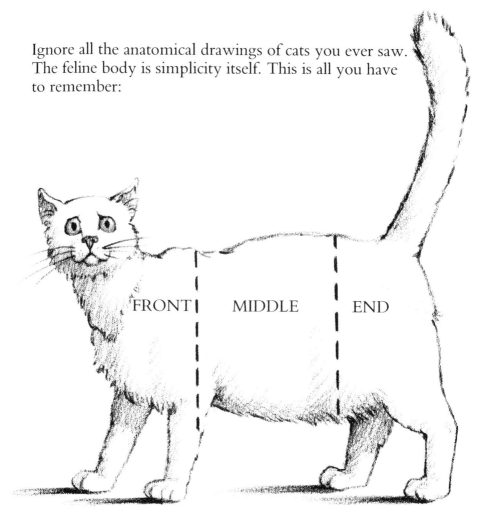

FRONT | MIDDLE | END

All three parts of a cat's body are put there for a reason.

The **front** of a cat is to encase his brain, the existence of which is a subject of some controversy among cat owners but not cats.

The **middle** takes up the largest area of our body, and for a good cause. It is here that the stomach—one of the busiest organs in our body—is situated.

The **end** supports our tail and gives us a base on which to sit.

To summarise:

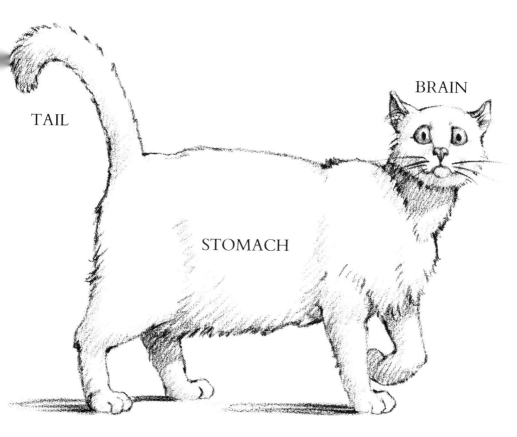

TAIL

BRAIN

STOMACH

Attached to our body are our **feet**. These pedal extremities enable us to stand up or—if we think the idea has merit—move from point A to point B, as, for example, from the kitchen to the living room.

Our feet are superior to those of any other living being. Study these pictures and see for yourself.

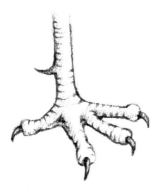 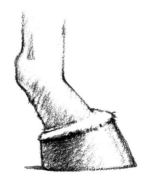 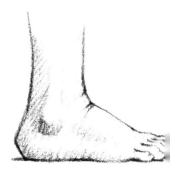

BIRD	HORSE	MAN
Cannot walk on its toes as lightly as we can	Can run on the ground but has difficulties climbing a curtain.	The clumsiest feet of all. Unable to grab and lift up even the simplest of objects, such as a pillow or dead mouse off the floor.

OUR FRONT PAWS are one of nature's wonders. Claws enable us to hold on to any object, turn upholstery into shreds, pull off bedspreads, and leave scratch marks on furniture, wallpaper and people's necks. We can retract or extend our claws, depending on our mood, our intentions, and the size of the enemy confronting us. The only missing part is a middle finger with which to give the sign—this we wish we had.

MISSING FINGER

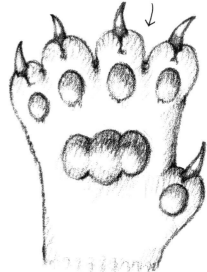

Padded feet allow us to make progress on uncertain terrain.

Claws keep us from slipping.

Firm footing—and persistence—makes it possible for us to seize upon and take possession of an object much heavier than ourselves.

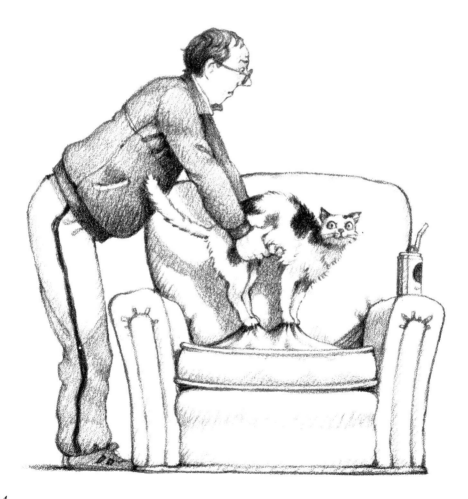

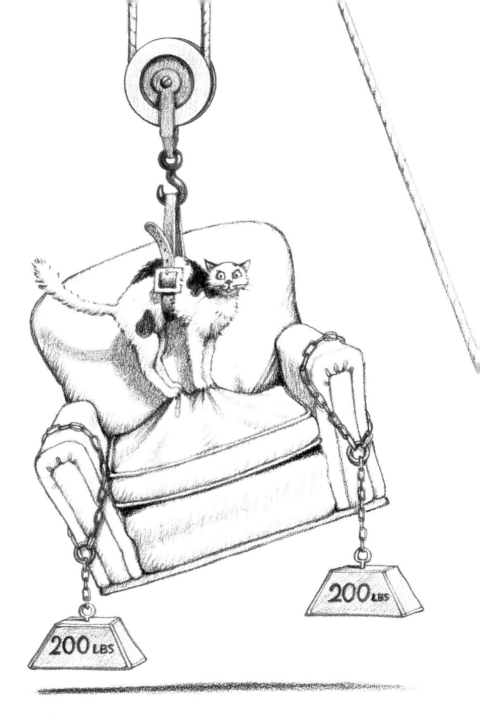

Every cat needs one or several scratching posts to keep his claws sharp, his self-esteem intact.

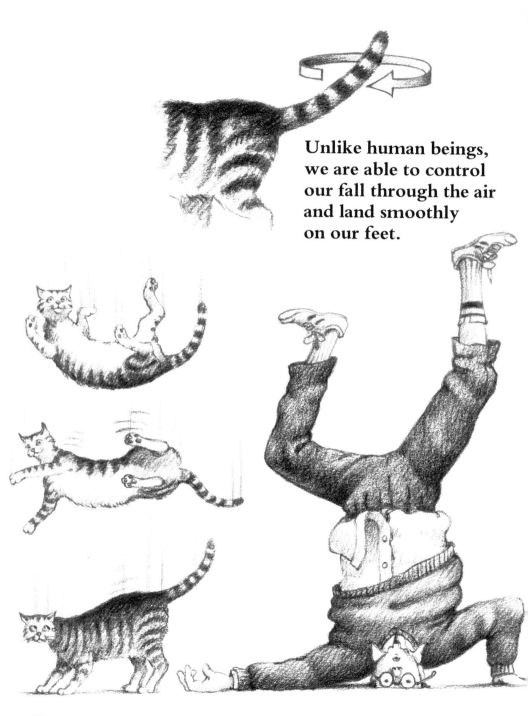

Unlike human beings,
we are able to control
our fall through the air
and land smoothly
on our feet.

Our highly developed **sensory organs**, strategically located in and around our head, help us to cope with our owner.

Our **ears** can be pointed forward, pricked up or—most importantly—pressed against the head effectively to block unwanted noise, such as our owner's voice.

We keep our **eyes** either half or wholly closed except when dinner is being served, there is a good programme on television, or a dog has just entered the room.

Our **nose** is just above the mouth to sniff at food, to push against our owner's face, or wrinkle in disgust.

Our **mouth** allows food to enter the body, a vital function.

Nocturnal vision makes it possible for us to get in front of our owner on the way to the kitchen in the dark.

Our hearing apparatus enables us easily to distinguish between pleasant sounds and just plain noise.

SOUNDS WE APPRECIATE:

MOZART'S CONCERTO FOR PIANO NO. 21 IN C
DOG WHINING
SHARPENING OF CLAWS AGAINST WALLPAPER
CAN BEING OPENED
CALL FOR DINNER

NOISES WE CAN DO WITHOUT:

SNORING
DOG BEING PRAISED
ALARM CLOCK RINGING
RAP MUSIC
THE WORD "NO"

QUIET
PLEASE

These scent signals cause our nose to quiver. Sense of smell saves us from having to get up and walk all the way to the source.

VEAL CORDON BLEU

LASAGNA ALLA BOLOGNESE

LEMON SOLE MEUNIÈRE

SPECIAL CHICKEN SCARPARIELLO

CAESAR SALAD

TOFU TEMPURA

MINCED FILET MIGNON CACCIATORE

SHRIMP SALAD PLATTER

DOUBLE LAMB CHOP

Much has been made of the fact that we rarely if ever smile.

Maybe so. But then . . . what is there to smile about?

Dogs smile. They smile at their owner's one-liners, funny or not. They smile when their chin is chucked, their ears are scratched, they are paid a compliment, the owner makes a face. Does that mean dogs have a better sense of humour? We certainly don't think so. We think they smile because they feel it is expected that they do so. Such behaviour is beneath our dignity.

If there is one thing we have learnt—knowledge passed down from one generation to the next—it's that it is wiser to keep our opinions to ourselves. Facial expressions are best avoided. They may be misinterpreted.

Should we wish to vent our feelings, we prefer the use of body language. Always, we make an effort to keep our messages simple enough for anyone to understand.

This cat is frustrated with his owner.

This cat is ready to climb the wall.

This cat has HAD IT.

3

See Cat Run

O wners keep asking: What is it that compels cats to run all over the house, far exceeding the legal speed limit?

Here are just some of the questions hurled at us as we cover the distance:

"Just where do you think you're going?"

"What's the rush?"

"Have you completely lost your senses?"

Actually, we have good reasons for zipping through space in such a hurry. Speed saves time: there are only so many hours a day to see if anything important took place while we were sleeping on the couch. We like to be kept right up to date.

The following pages should speak for themselves.

For starters, we jump on the chair.

Table comes next.

We land on the floor in preparation for another take-off.

No obstacle is too great for us.

We climb the curtains to get a better view.

Dish filled with cat food offers no excuse to slow down, not if real dinner is only a short hop away.

Time has come to get some rest after an arduous workout.

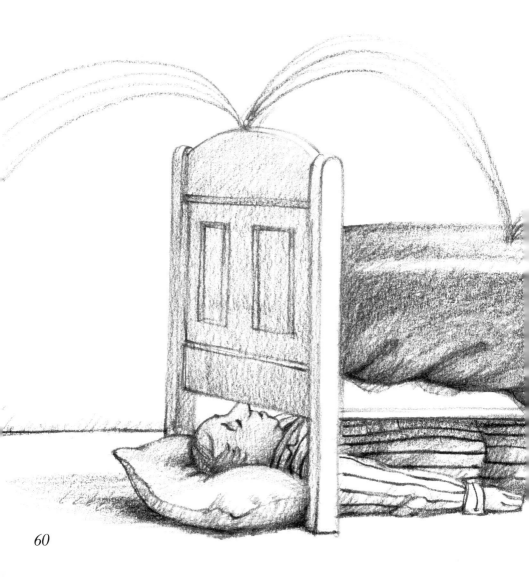

4

Are You Qualified to Own a Cat?

C at owners come in different sizes, shapes and temperament. No one knows that better than we do.

This chapter should help you to understand the way we think. As usual, we follow the dictates of plain common sense. There are two things that we take into account as we move into a home:

The Person.

The Place.

Obviously, the latter takes precedence over the former. This is not to suggest that we pay no attention to the occupant. It is only that we know from experience that sooner or later he will see things our way. All we have to do is show that we care. To wit:

Show up at least once a day: at lunch.
Show up twice a day: at lunch and dinner.
Show up three times a day: at lunch, dinner and bedtime.

The Place presents more of a problem. It is more resistant to change, to our efforts to make improvements; i.e., move the pillows from the bedroom to the living room, unmake the bed, overturn the waste-paper basket.

Actually, when it comes to living accommodations, we are easy to please. The rooms don't have to be large, or even numerous. This floor plan, for example, suits us perfectly:

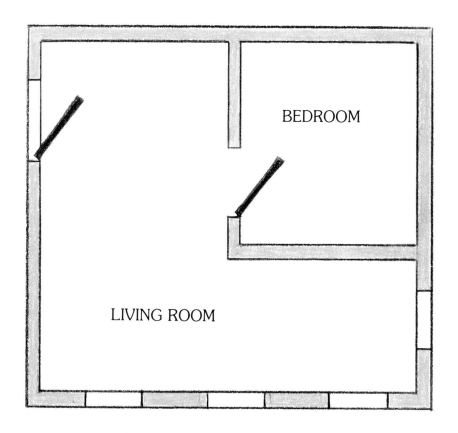

These are the items of importance:

Doors. They should swing open easily, providing access to every room and cupboard.

Windows. Large enough to provide a view of the sky, birds, clouds, other cats.

Kitchen Cupboards. Place for food for immediate consumption.

Refrigerator. Place for food for future consumption.

Bed. Large enough for the owner and his cat.

Dining Table. With a chair reserved for us.

Cupboard space. For much needed privacy.

Television. Remote control that allows us to change channels without having to get up from the living room sofa.

CAT'S FAVOURITE
TELEVISION PERSONALITIES

Delia Smith

Keith Floyd

Michael Barry

Gary Rhodes

Clement Freud

CAT'S LEAST FAVOURITE
TELEVISION PERSONALITY

Mr Motivator

HOW TO CHOOSE THE CAT JUST RIGHT FOR YOU

In the shop window, all cats look very much the same: cuddly, adorable, irresistible. We see to that; the ploy has served us well through the years.

Some owners, however, insist that beauty is only fur-deep. They want to know more about the cat they are about to take home. The animal may have deep-seated hidden problems, they say, if not physical, then emotional.

Here's a bit of friendly advice: To make sure that you have made the right choice, watch for these telltale clues while examining the cat you took a liking to:

He gives you a suspicious glare
He makes a face when he looks at you
He bites your fingers as you lovingly pat him on the head
He scratches your nose when you try kissing him
He slips out of your hand

If this is the way he behaves, you are in luck. Such behaviour is a sign of a normal, well-adjusted cat.

But which?

Perhaps a cat isn't for you at all.
Consider the alternatives.

Part Two

THEM, THE OWNERS

*Everthing your cat knows about you
without even having to ask.*

The fact that we have learnt to keep opinions of our owners to ourselves does not mean we don't have any.

A DISCLAIMER: Our owners may be either men or women, so the pronouns "he" and "she" are used arbitrarily in the following pages. This is not to suggest preference. We cats do not engage in any forms of discrimination, gender or otherwise, so long as the food is good.

5

The Hugger

Huggers do not just pick up and hold us in their arms as you would normally expect. They hug us, they squeeze us, they strangle us.

This is the Hugger's way of showing love and affection. Whatever resistance she encounters, she pretends not to notice. She is firm in her conviction that her embrace represents the high point of our day; we could hardly wait for her to pick us up.

We do our best to let her know that this is not the case. Sometimes we succeed. More often, we do not. But we keep trying just the same.

HOW TO COPE

1. Inhale deeply
2. Hold your breath, puff up chest
3. Twist the body, shake
4. Blow out chest
5. Wriggle loose, land on floor
6. Run

IF NEED BE, MEET FORCE WITH FORCE.
SOME OF THE MORE POPULAR TECHNIQUES WE USE:

The Choke. Encircle owner's neck with front legs, thrash with the other two.

The Ear Nip. Bite one, or better still, *both* earlobes.

The Free-for-all. Extend claws, bare teeth, scratch, bite.

The Dracula Drain. Go for the blood.

HUGGERS HUG WHEN

They greet us at the front door upon returning home

They wake up to a nightmare next to us in bed

Listen to soft music

They meet us at the door as the police finally bring us home after an intensive three-week search

FAVOURITE PHRASES

Come to your mummy, dear.

Let's shake hands, okay?

Is a little kiss from you too much to ask?

Feel my heart. Hey, I feel yours.

6

The Live-Alone

The Live-Alone is the first to admit that the most important person in her life is her cat. She could be right.

This is not to imply that sharing room and board with the Live-Alone is never without problems—it never is living with any human being. The point is that, by comparison, sharing a home with this owner isn't all that bad.

For one thing, territorial disputes occur rarely, if ever. The Live-Alone is willing to face the facts: namely, that her cat always comes first.

That's because, whatever the differences, they are easier to settle with only one person representing the opposite side. With no squealing babies interrupting the conversation, no one else in the family butting in, no roommates demanding equal time, this owner is willing to hear us out, and act promptly upon our complaints.

HOW TO RECOGNISE THE LIVE-ALONE

Calls her cat "best friend"

Tells her friends there's nothing in the world like the companion-ship of a cat

Remembers her cat's birthday

Names her cat in her Last Will as the prime beneficiary

WHAT TO DO WHEN THE LIVE-ALONE HAS VISITORS

Find out who is allergic to cat. Jump onto his lap, brush against his nose.

Make a gift of a dead mouse.

Eat the flowers someone brought.

Yawn when someone tells a joke. Then walk away.

FAVOURITE PHRASES

Where have you been all my life?

It's just you and me, isn't it?

Where would I be without you?

79

THE FELINE EASY-ACCESS HOME

Soon to be introduced will be rooms furnished for our convenience:

1. **Ladder leading to top of bookcase.**

2. **Windows placed near the floor for quicker exit.**

3. **Sofa large enough to accommodate both owner and cat.**

4. **Door flaps to enable cat to move from one room to another with minimum effort.**

5. **Mousetrap to catch mouse ready to serve.**

6. **Refrigerator to open electronically at the touch of a paw.**

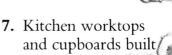

7. **Kitchen worktops and cupboards built for easy access.**

8. **Steps leading to top of rubbish bin.**

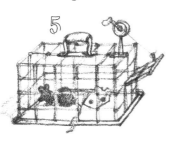

7

The Expert

The term "expert" causes us to snigger. This owner actually believes he *knows* all there is to know about the feline species.

Words rarely fail him when talk turns to his favourite topic. He is able to identify the various breeds, complete with their land of origin, genetic history, physiognomy, length of tail. He is thoroughly familiar with the recommended dosages of vitamin A, D, E and B_{12}, purported to add another nine years of life to our already established nine. Our jaws become "lower mandibles" to this owner, our feet "metacarpals", our meowing "vocalisation". If all this fails to impress us cats, the same cannot be said of his feline-owning friends.

We usually let the Expert go on and on without interrupting him. As often as not, we simply leave the room and head for the kitchen or bedroom beyond hearing distance. Still holding forth, he is unlikely to notice our absence.

HOW TO RECOGNISE THE EXPERT

Keeps at least six Ultimate Cat Books on his shelf

Puts through emergency call ("my cat is sneezing") to the vet late at night

He doesn't just "have" a cat—he "breeds" him

FAVOURITE PHRASES

Malayan cats did not originate in Malaya.

There are no cats in Antarctica.

Australia had no cats until man brought them there. The first cat show was held at the Crystal Palace in 1871.

Here's how to transport a cat from one place to another.

IMPROPER   IMPROPER

PROPER

1. Siren
2. Rotating Beacon
3. Ceiling Fan
4. Bulletproof Window
5. Stereo Speaker
6. Cushions
7. Divan

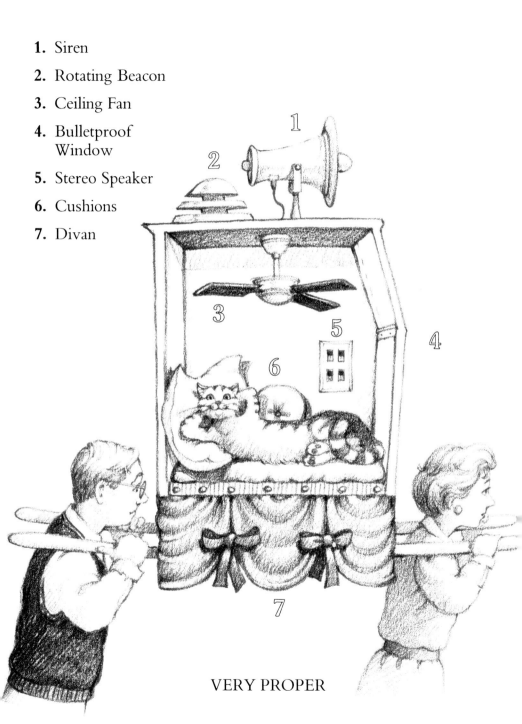

VERY PROPER

8

The Animal Lover

His generous, open-minded approach to all members of the animal kingdom, be they small or large, tall or short, flat or round, smart or truly dumb, touches the heart. Crawl, swim, fly, climb or walk on four legs—it makes no difference to this owner. All living things are equal in God's eyes, he proclaims loudly, in the face of overwhelming evidence to the contrary.

Not surprisingly, his irrational approach to pet ownership brings up a number of problems at home, what with so many animals of different persuasion under the same roof. Territorial disputes are more the rule than the exception. As often as not, they are decided based on the owner's—not our—concept of equitable distribution.

HOW TO RECOGNISE THE ANIMAL LOVER

He vacuums the carpet at least twice a day, changes upholstery four times a year, replaces indoor plants every day

He calls his live-in animals "my family"

His neighbours and former spouse refer to his place as the "local zoo"

WHAT TO DO IF OTHER ANIMALS TAKE UP SPACE ON THE LIVING ROOM SOFA OR IN FRONT OF THE TELEVISION

Hiss

Spit

Claw

Bite

All of the above

FAVOURITE PHRASES

Who ate my canary?

Who ate my pet fish?

Who ate my parakeet?

Who ate my hamster?

Without doubt, the most intrusive of all house pets are dogs.

Not only do they take up space—in front of the television, for example—but socially they have no redeeming value whatsoever.

9

The Dog Fancier

This owner deserves special mention. He is an Animal Lover all right, but with one important difference. He sees the dog as the animal at the top of the evolutionary ladder, and a role model to his cat.

He has "facts" to back up his contention. For example, he will point at his dog's willingness—nay, eagerness—to respond to his master's voice instantly and with a smile.

We don't agree that this kind of behaviour suggests keenness of mind. It happens to be just the other way round—it requires no particular imagination to do what one is told.

Dogs lag behind us in every way. As a matter of fact, the gap between us and our canine roommates, both from a physical and mental point of view, is considerable. Hence, the term "underdog".

Consider the following:

DOG	CAT
Stays on the floor when pushed off the bed	Will walk round the bed and jump back instantly
Makes an effort to keep awake while spoken to	Goes to sleep, though with his eyes open as if paying attention
Will eat at given times of the day, following a fixed schedule	Will eat whenever hungry, day or night—especially at night
Acts as a hunting companion to man	The last thing he would want is to have his owner interfere with his chasing after prey
Will pull a sledge	Prefers to sit on top of it
Tries to cheer up owner if need be Does not object to leash	Expects owner to cheer him up Tolerates leash only if he can lead the way
Answers to call	Pays no attention to being called, except at dinnertime.

HOW TO RECOGNISE THE DOG FANCIER

Praises the dog in cat's presence

Smiles back at his dog

Wants his dog and cat to be "good friends"

FOUR WAYS TO MAKE DOG'S LIFE MORE MISERABLE

Take his place on the bed

Eat his food

Jump in the owner's lap before he does

Blame dog for everything

FAVOURITE PHRASES

My dog *listens* to me. How come you never do?

There's a lot you could learn from my dog.

This home belongs to *both* of you, you hear?

Why can't you be more like a dog?

10

The Little One

Any addition to the household is a traumatic experience for us, creating new stress in what has already proved to be a stressful existence. This person can't even take care of his most basic needs. He lacks all social graces. Not only is he competing for attention—he wants it all.

He has yet to learn to keep his voice at a normal level; his idea of a dialogue is to scream out loud. His vocal presence interferes with our sleep at night and, worse still, during the day.

The situation is all the more surprising in view of the fact that, just as with dogs, we are superior to human infants in more ways than one. Consider:

BABY	**CAT**

First few days

Cries a lot, except when asleep.	Doesn't waste time crying. When hungry, heads straight for his mother.

Three months

Able to sit up but not for long.	Able to walk across the room, lie down on the sofa, windowsill, owner's bed.
Fixes eyes on a moving object, but has trouble grasping it.	Has no difficulty in capturing a moving object, especially if it's edible.

Seven months

At long last he has learnt to get hold of a moving object and bring it to his mouth.	Considers putting his hind legs in his mouth stupid.

One year

Crawls around on all fours, slowly and with difficulty.	Runs around freely.

Two years

Begins to understand what is being said. Tries standing up on his hind legs but has a problem keeping his balance.	Understands everything that is being said. This enables him to listen to instructions and ignore them.

HOW TO COPE WITH THE LITTLE ONE

Pull off his socks

Eat his food

Take over his cot

Offer him a friendly handshake with claws fully extended

Steal his blanket

WHAT TO DO WHEN THE LITTLE ONE SCREAMS

Try outshouting him

Lie across his face

Hide in the cupboard and cover your ears

Leave home for the next twenty-one years

FAVOURITE LAST WORDS OF THE LITTLE ONE'S PARENTS

You two are going to get along just fine.

Meet your new brother (or sister).

How about a nice photograph of both of you together?

11

The Cat Collector

To this owner the entire animal kingdom consists of only two subdivisions: (1) cats and (2) non-cats. It is the former where her interest happens to be.

It's not that this owner doesn't understand us. The problem with the Cat Collector lies elsewhere. She is convinced that her cat is happiest in company with other cats—the more, the merrier.

That being the case, she is poised to add to her ever-growing feline assembly anywhere, at any time. Any cat she encounters outside her home, in the street, in the park, or even in the neighbour's front garden, meets her definition of a "stray" looking for a home: hers.

And so, given enough time, the cat who was there first loses his special status. There will be others just like him making exactly the same kind of demands.

HOW TO RECOGNISE THE CAT COLLECTOR

Able to carry up to three cats under each arm

Speaks of her cats as "brothers" and "sisters" even when no such family ties exist

Calls every one of her cats an "individual"

HOW TO COPE WITH THE NEWCOMER

Ignore him

Finish his dish of food before he gets to it

Fight with the other cats and let the owner know it is they who started it

HOW TO STAND OUT FROM THE CROWD

Be first in the kitchen when owner brings home the groceries

Be first at the dinner table

Be first in the owner's bed

Be last to leave the owner's bed in the morning

FAVOURITE PHRASES

. . . Well, well. The gang's all here.

Run along and play with your friends.

Look who I brought home this time.

Meet your new friend, everybody!

We're just one big happy family.

12

The Braggart

This owner ranks high on our list.

To hear the Braggart tell it, there is no cat like his cat. He has more pictures of his cat in his wallet than credit cards. With camera in hand, he is predisposed to put his cat's every move on film. See the animal leaping over furniture, sleeping in the kitchen sink, sharing baby's milk bottle, joining the rest of the family at the dinner table.

Braggarts have a ubiquitous presence; you'll find them wherever people gather: pet food section in the supermarket, queues forming in front of the bank cashier's window, at a bus stop. It is easy to strike up a conversation with the Braggart—he usually starts it. The problem is how to stop it.

HOW TO RECOGNISE THE BRAGGART

Introduces his cat by name to visitors at his house

Prefers colour photographs to black-and-white to show off his cat's singular markings

Claims his cat follows his every instruction

BRAGGART'S SEVEN FAVOURITE NAMES FOR CATS

Napoleon

Moses

Einstein

Winston Churchill

Shakespeare

Madonna

Robert Maxwell

THE BRAGGART'S CAT

is smarter than anyone else's

has just set new world records in high jumping, long jumping, number of mice caught

could win top honours in any cat show if he would only be entered

understands three languages including English

FAVOURITE PHRASES

There is no cat like my cat.

This picture doesn't do him justice.

You must come and meet my cat one of these days.

Sometimes I think my cat is a *person!*

13

The Flat
Dweller

All Flat Dwellers insist that cats make the best pets of all for anyone living in an enclosed area. Should you question their position, you will be met with an icy stare—you just don't get it.

Deep inside their heart, Flat Dwellers often experience twinges of guilt, however. What makes them feel that way is that they are responsible for keeping their cats behind walls. No trees to climb, no fallen trunks to leap over, no hiding places—life in the wild. The Flat Dweller can only hope that somehow we will be able to survive the change.

In point of fact, flat living suits us perfectly. The roof over our head keeps the rain out. Food is no farther than the supermarket around the corner. And, most importantly, no longer must we work for a living.

HOW TO RECOGNISE THE FLAT DWELLER

Apologises for lack of adequate space

Buys us cat exercisers

Takes us for long walks

WHAT TO LOOK FOR WHEN LOOKING OUT OF THE WINDOW

Birds

More birds

Dogs

Any moving object

Other cats

General weather condition

FAVOURITE PHRASES

If we only had a garden . . .

Shall I turn up the heating for you?

Shall I turn down the heating for you?

Let's watch television, shall we?

What the Flat Dweller feels she
cannot give her cat in way of space, she
makes up for with expressions of love.

The Chest Massage fills lungs with air, helping the cat to regain full consciousness after a long sleep

The Back Massage stimulates blood flow

110

All cats enjoy a good massage. It makes up for the lack of exercise—if not the cat's, then the owner's.

The Paw Massage is like a friendly handshake. Owner shakes paws vigorously, cat limpidly accepts

The Head Massage encourages mental activity, if any

14

The Mouser

The Mouser lives in the past. He still believes chasing after mice is part of cats' job description.

He has visions of his cat stalking his target, muscles tensed, whiskers quivering with anticipation, this followed by a blood-curdling shriek as he pounces upon his prey.

It's hard to convince the Mouser that those days are gone. Alas, today we have mousetraps, boxes of Bromadialone, the Man from Rentokil, to take care of that sort of work. Call it progress, if you will.

We have better things to do than try to catch creatures running in the opposite direction. Something less swift on foot is more to our liking: Whiskas, Kit-e-Kat, Sheba come to mind.

HOW TO RECOGNISE THE MOUSER

Has motorised mouse for cat to practise on

His favourite nursery rhyme is: *Pussy Cat, Pussy Cat,*
What did you there?
I frightened a little mouse
Under the chair.

His favourite story has to do with "Mickey," a tabby, who reputedly killed more than 22,000 mice during his lifetime according to the *Guinness Book of World Records*.

HOW TO REACT TO THE MOUSER'S FAVOURITE STORIES ABOUT MOUSE-CATCHING CATS

Pretend you're paying attention

Smile

Nod in approval

Take a nap

WHAT TO DO WHEN THE MOUSE APPEARS

Jump off the sofa, circle the room

Stare at the mouse

Run round the room twice

Run round the room three times

Extend your claws as if ready for action

Nothing

FAVOURITE PHRASES

God created cats to hunt mice.

After the mouse, cat!

Wake up, cat!
Whatever happened to the good old-fashioned work ethic?

15

The Jewish (Italian, Greek, etc.) Mother

When it comes to food, sleep and the meaning of life, just ask the Jewish (Italian, Greek, etc.) Mother. She *knows*.

This owner is everywhere all the time. Her figure looms large in the kitchen preparing the next meal. She will pull the blanket up covering our face to make sure we're not about to catch a life-threatening disease, like a common cold. She will keep an eye on us through the window to ensure we don't risk life and limb by climbing too far up a tree. Or go and chase an animal through a field. Or get into an argument—with a dog.

We are smart enough to accept the Jewish (Italian, Greek, etc.) Mother's ubiquitous presence and try to make the best of it. There's no way of avoiding it, anyway.

HOW TO RECOGNISE THE JEWISH (ITALIAN, GREEK, ETC.) MOTHER

Shops at health food stores for pet food

Thinks no other cat is good enough to date hers

Insists her cat keeps curfew hours

HOW TO COPE

Turn up your nose at gefilte fish (spaghetti and meat sauce, stuffed vine leaves, etc.) and ask for *your* favourite dish

Ignore owner's objections and keep seeing other cats regardless of their race, colour or national origin

Refuse to stay at home on a rainy day

FAVOURITE PHRASES

You're not to leave this house on an empty stomach.

Be home by eleven.

I'm doing this for your own good.

Eat your dinner, dear.

One day you'll thank me for this.

16

The Playmate

The Playmate thinks we are toys with movable parts, no batteries required.

She enjoys playing with us whenever and wherever she feels like it.

It's difficult, if not impossible, to persuade the Playmate to ask us again some other time, perhaps, say a month from now. Perish the thought. Crying "Playtime!" this owner will raise us high up in the air, wake us, run around the room in circles expecting us to do the same.

Having no other choice, we often pretend to welcome her exuberant company, hoping all the while she will tire out before we do.

HOW TO RECOGNISE A PLAYMATE

She thinks running around the room is fun

She thinks jumping up and down is fun

She thinks crawling under the furniture is fun

She thinks rolling a ball in our direction is fun

PLAYMATE'S IDEA OF CAT'S FAVOURITE TOYS

Cat tree

Cat exercisers

Wriggly cat toys

Plastic kitten gym

Rubber mouse

CAT'S FAVOURITE TOYS★

Rolls of toilet paper (64 feet or more)

Square pillows

Round pillows

Pillows of any shape

Bed cover

Tropical fish

Canary

Small dog

Any toy that belongs to the child

★All to be found right here at home

FAVOURITE PHRASES

Catch!   **Roll over!**

Jump!   **Peek-a-boo!**

APT
6A

124

17

The Nine-to-Fiver

Nine-to-Fivers leave home in the morning blowing a kiss and return at the end of the day just as effusive, smiling broadly as they try to hide their guilt for leaving us at home alone all day. They usually appear at the door in the evening complete with new toys and plenty of food to atone for their absence.

We appreciate such demonstrations of love, of course, even encourage them. We're not going to tell the Nine-to-Fiver the truth: there is plenty to do at home, with or without her. This would be a typical schedule:

7:30–8:30 A.M.	Move from bed to living room sofa.
8:30–8:35 A.M.	Move from living room sofa to windowsill.
8:35–9:35 A.M.	Move from windowsill to kitchen sink
9:35–10:30 A.M.	Move from kitchen sink to top drawer of dressing-table.

10:30 A.M.	Check the food supply in the kitchen cupboard.
10:31–11:00 A.M.	Take nap on the top shelf of the kitchen cupboard.
11:00 A.M.	Try climbing the curtains. If you don't succeed at first, try again.
11:00 A.M.**–12:45** P.M.	Rest. Climb under bed cover in the bedroom.
12:50 P.M.	Rearrange pillows. Throw the ones you don't need on the floor, strew them around, hide some under the bed.
1:00 P.M.	Pull off the bed cover, spread it out under the bed.
1:01 P.M.	Try to climb the curtains again, this time in the bedroom.
1:05 P.M.	Stop to admire your image in the mirror.
1:07 P.M.	Remove bedroom lampshade, pounce on it hard.
1:30 P.M.	Pull out wires in back of television set, piece them together. Make sure owner will have to call outside help to have it fixed.
2:00 P.M.	Visit bathroom, use litter tray. Spread contents in the bathtub, on the floor.
2:30 P.M.	Flush toilet.
3:15 P.M.	Take all toothbrushes to the living room, lay them out on the carpet.
4:00 P.M.	Talk to the parakeet, insult him, lick your lips in front of him. If he keels over from a heart attack, throw his body in the rubbish bin.
4:30–5:30 P.M.	Rest.

126

5:30–6:00 P.M.	Sharpen your claws on wallpaper, on the carpet, on the television screen.
6:00–6:30 P.M.	Eat anything edible—or inedible. Finish off the indoor plants left over from yesterday.
6:30–7:00 P.M.	Rest.
7:00 P.M.	Greet owner at the door, pretend you're glad to see her again.
7:15 P.M.	Get underfoot while she is preparing dinner. Leap on the kitchen worktop. Be where least expected.
7:30 P.M.	When left alone in the kitchen, turn on tap, flood the floor.
7:35–8:30 P.M.	Join owner at the dinner table.
8:35–10:00 P.M.	Watch old movies on television.
10:00–10:15 P.M.	Retire. Precede owner to bedroom, get under the blanket before she does.
10:15–10:30 P.M.	Plan next day's activities before going to sleep.

HOW TO RECOGNISE THE NINE-TO-FIVER

Announces her presence the moment she enters the room

Feels the need to apologise for not spending more time with her cat

Takes cat with her on holiday

HOW TO COPE

Pretend the gifts she brings you on her return home are just what you always wanted

Look dejected when she leaves in the morning

Smile when she returns

WHAT TO DO WHEN THE NINE-TO-FIVER BRINGS WORK HOME FROM THE OFFICE

Sit on the top of her desk taking up as much room as possible

Rearrange her notes

Play with the computer disc

Hide her glasses

Catch up on your sleep inside her filing cabinet

Punch out your own message on the computer keyboard. Never mind errors in spelling.

FAVOURITE PHRASES

Did you miss me?

Hope you'll be all right without me.

Were we a good cat today?

I tried calling you . . .

18

The Chatterbox

Happiness to the Chatterbox is talking to her cat. For whatever reason, she believes that her cat makes an excellent listener, intent on her every word. She says she can tell that from watching her cat as he stares fixedly at her mouth, reading her lips.

Little does she know that through years of experience we have learnt the knack of looking interested even when we're not. We know how to sleep with our eyes open.

This is co-dependence at its best. Our owner needs someone to talk to. We need someone to prepare dinner for us.

and then . . . can you **believe it?** . . . I said, all right, all
right, I understand what you're trying to tell me . . . you
know I'm trying to be polite . . . It's my nature to be
that way . . . I suppose I picked that up from my mother . . .
well, maybe my father . . . **no, it was my mother . . .** she
was a **gentle soul . . .** always insisted we keep our temper
no matter what . . . **be nice**, she'd say . . . being nasty
doesn't work out, not **in the long run . . .** insults have a
way of coming back at you just when you least
expected. You tell that to my sister . . .
oh, my sister . . . I have
to tell you about
her . . . she was . . .
something else . . .

and then . . . can you **believe it**? . . . I said, all right, all right, I understand what you're trying to tell me . . . you know I'm trying to be polite . . . It's my nature to be that way . . . I suppose I picked that up from my mother . . . well, maybe my father . . . **no, it was my mother** . . . she was a **gentle soul** . . . always insisted we keep our temper no matter what . . . **be nice**, she'd say . . . being nasty doesn't work out, not **in the long run . . .** insults have a way of coming back at you just when you least expected. You tell that to my sister . . . oh, my sister . . . I have to tell you about **her . . .** she was . . . something else . . .

HOW TO RECOGNISE THE CHATTERBOX

Believes her cat's vocabulary matches hers

Keeps asking cat for an opinion on a wide variety of subjects

Is never lost for words

KEEPS TALKING TO HER CAT WHILE

Putting groceries away

Preparing dinner

Watering her plants

Giving cat a bath

Solving a crossword puzzle

Vacuuming the carpet

Eating dinner

HOW TO COPE

Hide under the living room sofa

Cover head with a pillow

Turn up the television volume

Leave the room

Leave town

CHATTERBOX'S QUESTIONS WE CAN DO WITHOUT

How do you like my new hairdo?

Just how old do you think I am? Now tell me the truth.

What day is it?

What time is it?

SUBJECTS WE DON'T MIND DISCUSSING

Location of sun patches on the carpet

Choice of television programmes

Feeding schedule

Sleeping schedule

SUBJECTS WE DO MIND DISCUSSING

Visit to the vet

Benefits of taking a bath

Work ethics

Basic training

Names for the new dog

Names for the new baby

FAVOURITE PHRASES

Speak to me.

As I told you before . . .

Don't you agree?

Why are you looking at me like that?

Shall we talk?

19

And Now . . . the Winner Is

STEPHEN BAKER is the author of twenty-two books, about equally divided between humorous best sellers like *How to Play Golf in the Low 120's, How to Live with a Neurotic Dog, How to Live with a Neurotic Cat*, and professional works such as *Systematic Approach to Advertising Creativity*. As a vice president and creative director of Cunningham Walsh (now N. W. Ayer), he was responsible for many well-known campaigns (he created the best known advertising slogan in the United States, "Let Your Fingers Do the Walking", for ATNT) and was twice nominated as Art Director of the Year. A former columnist for *Advertising Age*, he is now president of his own advertising and marketing consultant firm in New York City and Washington, D.C. Some of his best friends are cats.

ROGER ROTH is well known for his whimsical but close-to-life drawings. Starting out as a sign painter, his work today can frequently be seen in such major publications as the *New York Times*,, the *Wall Street Journal, Business Week*, and *Redbook*. He illustrated Nancy Milton's popular children's book *The Giraffe That Walked to Paris*, as well as *The Sign Painter's Dream*, which he also wrote himself. He lives in Princeton, New Jersey, with his dogs, cats, and whatever other animal decides to come in out of the cold.